Push Through and Don't Pass Out!

Discovering the Inner Strength of a Warrior

Jacqueline Y. Howard

Push Through and Don't Pass Out: Discovering the Inner Strength of a Warrior

ISBN: 978-1-954595-15-6

Library Congress Control Number: 2022902839

Printed in the USA

Duncanville, Texas

Published by Sparkle Publishing

www.sparklepublishing.net

Sparkle Publishing
Write. Publish. Sparkle.

Dedication

This book is dedicated to my loving husband, who has been my greatest encourager, as well as my incredible children and grandchildren. Thank you for your support.

Acknowledgments

To the many people that inspired me and encouraged me
to push through and not give up. Thank you.

Table of Contents

Introduction

My name is Jacqueline Lofton, but loved ones call me Jackie, and this is my story.

In 1967, at five years old, I began attending local Black Panther meetings with my dad. However, in time, Dad wanted us to live in a safer neighborhood, so we ended up moving from a lower-income area to a middle-class neighborhood. When I started at my new elementary school, it took me a while to adjust because it was my first-time attending school with white and Black students. My mother came to my school every day to take me home because I would find myself in trouble. I continued getting in trouble in high school and was constantly sent home from school until the 11th grade. People picked on me, called me names, and threatened to fight me after school, so I had decided to defend myself. I became a fighter, and as time went on, I became a problem child. I ran away from home, stayed at a friend's house, and hung out with bad influences.

At 15 years old, I got pregnant, but I did not know I was pregnant. I was in denial. One day, my mother, who is a nurse, asked me if I had my cycle. I lied and said yes. My mother knew I was lying, and she asked to see my pad to make sure I was on my cycle.

At that moment, I went into the bathroom and put ketchup on a pad. That did not go over well when she saw it. So, she set up a doctor's appointment for the next day, where I found out I was pregnant. My mother was disappointed, and when she told my father, he took it hard. "You're just a baby yourself," he kept repeating in angry disbelief.

The next day, my parents told me I would not be going to school. Instead, we left our house, and I was unsure of where we were going. Come to find out, they were taking me to an abortion clinic. At the clinic, the staff performed an ultrasound and discovered I was five months pregnant; however, the clinic only performed abortions for women up to three months pregnant.

The news scared me, and I asked the staff not to tell my parents. Obviously, they had to because I was a minor, and upon hearing the news, my father went off, cussing everybody out and taking his frustrations out on the staff. He was highly disappointed. Mom, on the other hand, was silent. The staff had told my father about another clinic downtown that performs abortions for women five to nine months pregnant. He did not hesitate, and we headed to that facility.

As soon as we entered the building, my father went to the receptionist's desk and said, "My daughter is five months pregnant, and I want her to have an abortion."

The receptionist informed my dad that the abortion procedure would cost $500, to which he gave her cash and confirmed my appointment for the following day.

Throughout this ordeal, my mother did not say a word. I was so disconnected from it all. I was lost. I knew I had brought shame and heartache to my family, but I did not know what to do. Whatever they wanted seemed to be my plan of action, too.

That same day, after going to the clinic, I rested at home and fell asleep. I had been sleeping for about two hours when my mom came into my room, woke me up, and said, "Jackie, I had a dream that you died on the table while having the abortion."

I looked at her in shock, as if to say, "Are you serious?"

"You need to tell your dad that you want to have the baby," Mom demanded.

"I don't want to tell Dad," I cried.

"He'll listen to you," Mom assured me.

"No, Mom, you're his wife, and he will listen to you," I said, refusing to succumb to the idea of telling my father that I wanted to keep the baby.

Despite my fear, I decided to tell him. I saw my dad peacefully sleeping on the sofa in the living room, and as I gently woke him, I mustered up the courage to say, "Dad, I want to have the baby."

He jumped to his feet, cursing and fussing, reminding me that I was just a baby. As Dad was in a rage, I looked at Mom, but she said nothing. He was so mad that he left the house, once again repeating, "She's just a baby herself!"

"Go back and lay down," Mom encouraged, and back to my room I went.

When Dad returned home later that day, he was calmer and seemed ready to talk. He told me that I could have the baby. At the time, I was so concerned about my parents' feelings that I hardly made time to process my emotions. That baby is now my oldest daughter. She was a wonderful baby, and she is a gift from God.

During my pregnancy, at the end of summer 1979, my father took me shopping for school clothes, which was especially helpful because I could not fit in any of my clothes. During that week, one of my sisters, ten years my senior, called my mother and was chit-chatting, yet due to shame, Mom did not tell her what was going on with me. Mom ended up calling her back to tell her the truth. She then asked Mom if I could live with her until I had the baby.

So, in my tenth-grade year, I moved from Atlanta, Georgia, to Syracuse, New York, where my sister resided. Notably, it was my first time flying on an airplane.

My oldest sister's faith is Islamic. She and her family are Muslim and taught me about family values and responsibility. Their family openly discussed life, enjoyed dinner together each night, prayed, and believed in discipline. They showed me a new side to family I had not seen or experienced, which I enjoyed.

I attended a mother-specific school, where pregnant teenage girls earn their education and take their baby with them once the child is born. When my daughter was born, I was thankful to take her to school with me because the facility had a nursery on campus, and I even worked there after school hours. I learned about parenting and taking on the responsibility to raise my daughter.

During that time, I saw broken and confused young ladies. They did not have the support I had, which I now see clear as day but had yet to fully appreciate at that point in my life. Many of the young mothers that I had attended school with had put their children up for adoption, and many of those mothers were white, whereas many of the Black mothers kept their babies but did not have a lot of support to raise their children.

I did very well in school, but shortly after I had my daughter, I started going downhill, returning to my old ways of smoking cigarettes and sneaking out to go to the club. I met a friend who was older than me, and when I started hanging with her, my life began on a downward spiral. I met her brother, and we started dating I would sneak out with him and go clubbing, while my friend watch my baby. I also became rebellious toward my sister, staying out late and lying about where I was going,

One day, my friend asked me to ride with her somewhere. I thought we were going to get cigarettes, but instead, we went to her boyfriend's house. When we walked into his house, she immediately went with him to his room, leaving me in the living room alone. Moments later, an older guy walked out and took my hand, and we talked for a few minutes.

He started kissing on my neck, and the next thing I knew, I was out of my clothes, having sex with a stranger. I could not believe what I had just experienced. I just had my daughter, she was four months old, and I was trying to remain celibate. After that incident, I felt severe discomfort and was bleeding and shocked at what just happened. As my friend and I got into her car and headed back to her house, I remained in a daze. The daze turned into anger because I started having thoughts about becoming pregnant again and did not know him or his name. So, I asked my friend to give me his phone number, but she gave me a random number that did not work. I felt violated, stupid, and set up. Shortly after that, my sister decided I needed to move back to Atlanta because I was out of control. So, I moved back with my parents.

Chapter One

1982

In 1982, I met my husband, John Howard. I just graduated from high school, and John had just lost his job at Omni International. Our paths crossed when we started working at the same restaurant. We worked together and dated for one year before I got pregnant with John III, our son. One day, we were riding in the car and decided to go ahead and find a justice of the peace to marry us. Aqueelah, my daughter, was three years old at the time. After picking her up from daycare, she fell asleep in the car and continued to sleep as we wed through the justice of the peace.

I knew I wanted to get married before John III was born, but about four months after becoming husband and wife, we experienced financial hardship and believed we were ready for divorce. God's timing was perfect, though, as we were invited to attend church with my niece. We decided to go, and we have been there since 1983—since I was 19 years old, and my husband was

22. Had we not attended church together, our lives would not be the same. God saved our marriage and showed us our purpose by attending Atlanta Metropolitan Church, now Metro City Church (MCC).

Chapter Two

2010

Every year, our church conference is held in Bogota, Columbia. In 2010, I was able to attend and was thrilled. The conference was excellent, and thousands had attended. When the conference was over, we headed to the airport, and about 20 people from my church got in line at the check-in counter. When I was at the ticket counter, they began experiencing problems pulling up my information. The other lines continued moving, and all my church family had boarded the plane. The airport agent was unable to figure out why I could not board. An interpreter told me I would have to go to a hotel and come back in the morning. So, I spent the night in a hotel that I was familiar with when I had visited a couple of years ago. My interpreter then took me to get a phone card to call my husband. The card worked for about two minutes, but I was able to let my husband know where I was and that I was alright. This situation was scary because I did not speak Spanish and had to rely on an interpreter.

The next day, on Saturday, I received a call from my interpreter that he could not take me to the airport, but he was sending someone else. Paul, my driver, was kind, and he was concerned for me, too. I arrived at the airport to find out that I could not depart on Saturday. I was instructed to come back on Sunday because they did not have any planes flying out until then. So, I needed to find somewhere to stay until Sunday. Paul was gracious enough to allow me to stay at his home.

"You can meet my mom," he said. "She attends International Mission in Bogota. My family will take care of you," he assured.

I was numb from the uncertainty and constant changes. I could not believe I was left in Bogota. Despite Paul's invitation, I told him I would stay at the airport. They had guards in place, so I figured it would be okay, but Paul told me it would not be safe. So, I took him up on his offer.

When I arrived at Paul's house, I said a quick prayer: "Lord, give me peace when I walk in this house."

Paul's home had a yellow wall in the living room area, and I knew that the Lord was answering me because I had a wall in my kitchen that was the same color. This was a comforting sign. Paul's mom was pleasant and encouraging, reassuring me that I am their family and to make myself at home. I felt at peace in their house.

On Sunday, the following day, I went back to the airport only to discover that my status had changed again, which is why I could not board the plane. My son worked at the Atlanta airport, so he had arranged my ticket for this trip, but a few months before my trip to Bogota, he got married, which affected my status. So, I could not leave on Sunday. However, I returned to Paul's home and ministered to Paul's family. They gave me a list of family members they wanted me to include in my prayers. It was a trying time, but the Lord put me with the best. Through this brief yet difficult period, I realized how everything in life would not always be in my control, yet those moments are faith-building, and I will always choose to trust God with all my heart and lean not on my own understanding (Proverbs 3:5).

Early Monday morning, I was back at the airport, and my ticket went through. I was officially headed back to Atlanta, feeling happy and grateful.

Chapter Three

2012

On March 21, 2012, I had an appointment to see a doctor because I felt something unusual in my stomach, specifically the lower right area. I noticed this strange feeling about one month prior, but the movement had slowed down. However, sometime during the second week of March, I felt a lump on my stomach. I also asked my husband to check it, and he encouraged me to set up a doctor's appointment.

During my appointment, the doctor examined me, and she said that she wanted to schedule a CT scan. The results showed a mass growing from my kidney and a spot on my pelvic bone. So, she referred me to a urologist for a bone scan.

At my urologist appointment, the doctor informed me that a mass was growing on my kidney, likely cancerous, and needed to be removed along with my kidney. To say I was shocked would be an understatement. However, I needed to make an immediate decision regarding a surgery date. Thankfully, my cancer was stage two when they removed my kidney. More importantly, I was determined to stay in faith. I wholeheartedly believed God would heal me.

On March 27th, I went to my bone scan appointment, to which they performed a hip biopsy. Thankfully, the results were negative. At that point, I could focus on my kidney issue.

My husband and I went back to see the doctor, and he showed us the CT scan where cancer had grown over my right kidney. I was told I needed surgery by the end of April. The appointment was scheduled for April 18th. The doctor had commended me for discovering my lump. Otherwise, the only way I would have known was if I saw blood in my urine, and in that case, my cancer would have been far more advanced. Thankfully, I never saw blood and was not in pain.

I had people praying for me along this journey—family, pastors, church family, and friends. I felt peace, love, and support. Also, spending time with God every day helped me focus on His Word, not the doctor's reports. I would not allow doubt and disbelief to determine my health.

On April 9th, I had my biopsy. It was an unfamiliar experience, and as a person that wants to know all the details, the unknown was difficult for me to process. So, in an effort to not self-diagnose, I stayed away from the internet (per my husband and older sister's wisdom) and did not second-degree my doctors. My faith had been in a place where I chose to believe the Lord over my diagnosis.

During that time, my faith was challenged. Something my daughter said to me that was shared with her by a friend was that when you do not know what to do, follow these steps: (1) have your daily devotion (journal), (2) declare God's Word, (3) be around people with great faith, (4) read the Word daily, and (5) meditate and memorize Scripture.

I am learning that it is a choice to think negative or positive. You will believe the lie or the truth. The lie is the devil's facts, and the truth is the Lord's promise. Believers must be sold out to the Lord. We are faced with serious challenges that require our faith, not flesh. We cannot win in our flesh:

For our struggle is not against flesh and blood, but against the rulers, against the powers, against the world forces of this darkness, against the spiritual forces of wickedness in the heavenly places (Ephesians 6:12 NASB).

Upon reading *The Dream Giver* by Bruce Wilkinson, I yet again realized that our gifts come with a price. We must refuse to buy into the lie that our struggles are too hard to conquer, or our wilderness is too difficult to navigate.

It is not too hard.

It is not too long.

Our tests in the desert are the best answers to your deepest desires and prayers. Therefore, you must decide: Will you permit God to do His work for as long as He wants in the way He wants to change you as deeply as He wants to prepare you for your big dream?

Amid my faith-building journey, I received the following Scriptures: Psalm 46:1, Psalm 54, and Romans 4:16. Additionally, John 10:10 reminds us that thieves come only to steal, kill, and destroy. He came so that we may have life and have it abundantly. God wants us to trust Him, not just believe Him. So, let go of what you are carrying that is not yours to carry and trust Him (Proverbs 22:4-5). All it takes is one opportunity for the enemy to advance. So, we as warriors must remain consistent in prayer, refusing to give the devil a chance to enter our hearts and minds. Remember, this fight is fixed, and He will bring you through this. Remain focused on Scripture, and "do not let them depart from your sight":

My son, pay attention to my words; Incline your ear to my sayings. They are not to escape from your sight; Keep them in the midst of your heart. For they are life to those who find them, And healing to all their body. Watch over your heart with all diligence, For from it flow the springs of life. Rid yourself of a deceitful mouth And keep devious speech far from you. Let your eyes look directly ahead And let your gaze be fixed straight in front of you. Watch the path of your feet, And all your ways will be established. Do not turn to the right or to the left; Turn your foot from evil. (Proverbs 4:20-27 NASB).*

Fear of kidney cancer was causing me to doubt God's love for me. I have always associated dreadful things with someone doing something wrong, yet I saw terrible things happen to good people. We live in an imperfect world of people with free will. Therefore, misfortune has nothing to do with God's doing, for His love remains steadfast.

Waiting places can feel painful and uncomfortable. When Jesus was dying on the cross, he called out to his Father, but his Father did not answer him because God knew His son had to go through this. Similarly, God had not answered me because I needed that experience at that time. Well, Jesus was victorious; he conquered death, and I was looking forward to what I would conquer throughout my life, which had included my illness.

I asked the Lord to help me stay focused on Him, that I would not stop doing His work, and to put a weapon in my hand to destroy the enemy. I had been waiting for Him to reveal that weapon to me. One day, I was talking with my supervisor about what God was doing in my life. As I was talking with her, my eyes were opened to see that the weapon was my belief, and my arsenal is authoring this book so that other eyes can be open, too. The Lord had told me to stop paying attention to my circumstances and stand on the promises of God. He will not tell you to ignore the facts. Instead, He wants you to accept reality so that when He performs His promises, you will know it was God. You must remain obedient. Even if you do not know God, you know people who do, and you will be encouraged and blessed. My pastor had once said people tend to learn faith in difficult situations, yet we should learn a lifestyle of believing in God. Those words resonated with me because we must remember God is good and deserves praise regardless of circumstances.

Dive into His Word and hold steady to His promises:

"As for God, His way is blameless. The word of the Lord is refined. He is a shield to all who take refuge in Him."

(Psalm 18:30 NASB)

"The afflictions of the righteous are many, but the LORD rescues him from them all."

(Psalm 34:19 NASB)

"Trust in the LORD and do good. Live in the land and cultivate faithfulness."

(Psalm 37:3 NASB)

"Call upon Me on the day of trouble; I will rescue you, and you will honor Me."

(Psalm 50:15 NASB)

"I shall delight in Your statutes. I will not forget Your word."

(Psalm 119:16 NASB)

"Plead my cause and redeem me. Revive me according to Your word."

(Psalm 119:154 NASB)

"A joyful heart is good medicine, But a broken spirit dries up the bones."

(Proverb 17:22 NASB)

"And blessed is she who believed that there would be a fulfillment of what had been spoken to her by the Lord."

(Luke 1:45 NASB)

"Submit therefore to God. But resist the devil, and he will flee from you."

(James 4:7 NASB)

"And I will say to myself, 'You have many goods stored up for many years to come; relax, eat, drink, and enjoy yourself!'"

(Luke 12:19 NASB)

"Therefore, I say to you, all things for which you pray and ask, believe that you have received them, and they will be granted you."

(Mark 11:24 NASB)

"There is no fear in love; but perfect love drives out fear, because fear involves punishment, and the one who fears is not perfected in love."

(1 John 4:18 NASB)

"Beloved, do not be surprised at the fiery ordeal among you, which comes upon you for your testing, as though something strange were happening to you; but to the degree that you share the sufferings of Christ, keep on rejoicing, so that at the revelation of His glory you may rejoice and be overjoyed."

(1 Peter 4:12-13 NASB)

"You are from God, little children, and have overcome them; because greater is He who is in you than he who is in the world."

(1 John 4:4 NASB)

"And so, having patiently waited, he obtained the promise."

(Hebrews 6:15 NASB)

"Let us hold fast the confession of our hope without wavering, for He who promised is faithful."

(Hebrews 10:23 NASB)

Chapter Four

2012

On June 3, 2012, as I was coming out of recovery from kidney cancer, I also lost my firstborn grandchild in a car accident, but God had saved the other three.

That night, my daughter Aqueelah called me to ask if I could pick her up from work because her husband had not picked her up yet. One of my daughter's co-workers was waiting with her but needed to leave. So, I told her I would come. When I arrived, we called my oldest granddaughter, Corliss, and my other granddaughter, Joi, yet they did not answer. Of course, I wondered why. So, we rode to their house to see if they were home. We also drove on the highway to see if there was an accident, and we happened to see a police car. My daughter and I had a gut feeling, but we did not speak about it. Aqueelah called her husband, and sure enough, he told her he was in an accident. Perhaps fear of the unknown, how quickly the situation transpired, or total shock, but he did not inform us of the kids' status. So, we called and told my husband what happened, and we asked him to call the hospital to see if the kids were there. Sure enough, they were at Egleston Hospital. My husband wanted us to come back home to get him and my middle son to go with us to the hospital.

On our way there, we did not have a good feeling, but I did not want to say anything until I found out the facts. One of my sons and his wife arrived at the hospital before us. When we got there, we discovered that my grandson's had minor injuries, but my second granddaughter, Joi, was in intensive care, and my oldest granddaughter, Corliss, was still at the scene of the accident.

At that point, I lost it. I called my pastor's wife and told her I could not handle this. None of this seemed real. Eventually, the police gathered us together and shared that Corliss had died on the scene. I remember saying that the enemy finally got her.

That moment was one of the most trying times for my family and me. I did not have any answers, and I could not help my daughter who had lost her first-born child. Corliss was like my child. She was my greatest cheerleader, and she believed and supported me if no one else did. I could do no wrong in her eyes. She was one of a kind, yet we had to accept that Corliss had passed.

My daughter could not go home because the media had surrounded her house. At that point, we decided our daughter would stay with us. In the meantime, my husband, sons, daughters, and I prayed the blood prayers over Joi who had trauma to her brain. Joi remained in the hospital while we had Corliss' funeral. Our grandson's, thankfully, came through it all with minor injuries. Joi, however, was in the hospital for three months. She had to learn how to talk, walk, and eat again. She did not remember us, which was painful to endure. When Joi was released from the hospital, she began recovering very well, yet she was out of school for a year. Thankfully, her school had sent teachers to their house to help her catch up in her classes.

November 27, 2012

I feel so stupid. I woke up saying, "God, I feel like the enemy got the best of us. My granddaughter is gone. We have been faithful followers of Christ, yet I feel defeated."

My son-in-love was still coming around, but it was a struggle, especially with Joi's memory loss. Because of the brain injury, she would curse and sometimes say inappropriate comments. She had no filter on her mouth. The grandsons were good, but it had been a struggle losing Corliss. We were standing in faith, but I didn't see any changes, only that we needed to process losing Corliss and Joi's physical health. I felt defeated like the enemy won. So, why fight? Why dream and believe when anything can come along and change your life forever? I needed to know that my granddaughter's death was not in vain. I did not know how long it would take to get back to a place of joy and peace, but I knew everything would work itself out for good, yet I was sad and felt hopeless and defeated. I felt like that accident could have been prevented.

"Can I surrender my all to You again? I do not want to be disappointed. I feel like my fight is gone and not as strong as it used to be. I feel fragile in my faith, but I am pressing on and believing, yet I need to be healed, and only You can heal me," I had cried.

During that time of journaling, I also prayed daily for healing over Joi and for my strength. The following Scriptures often carried me through:

"When you pass through the waters, I will be with you; And through the rivers, they will not overflow you. When you walk through the fire, you will not be scorched, Nor will the flame burn you."

(Isaiah 43:2 NASB)

"Who pardons all your guilt, Who heals all your diseases."

(Psalm 103:3 NASB)

"'For I will restore you to health And I will heal you of your wounds,' declares the LORD, 'Because they have called you an outcast, saying: 'It is Zion; no one cares for her.'"

(Jeremiah 30:17a NASB)

"Is anyone among you sick? Then he must call for the elders of the church and they are to pray over him, anointing him with oil in the name of the Lord; and the prayer of faith will restore the one who is sick, and the LORD will raise him up, and if he has committed sins, they will be forgiven him."

(James 5:14-15 NASB)

Between reading Scripture, praying, and receiving encouraging words from loved ones, I tapped back into the strength of my faith.

This poem was given to me by a pastor who was friends with our pastor. Although we have lost contact, these words still resonate with me:

Though it's been rough for you, My Word will see you through. Though the times have been hard, I am still on watch and on guard. Though your tears may have a steady flow, trust Me I know. Though the pain seems too much to bear, sometimes you wonder if I really care. Listen to the still, small voice, for you will always have a choice to believe that I am there for you, to believe I will always come through. Although the pain is so intense, nothing seems to make any sense. Please know that I will take care of you; there will be times when I will carry you. Though you are in the thick of it, please know that I am in the midst of it. Though a cloud hovers over you, My grace is still enough for you!

I began pushing through, not passing out. The Word in all its forms helped me to see that the bigger picture was about her life, not her death. I continued to press on.

2013

We continued to believe in God and seek His favor, hoping that my son-in-love would receive mercy and grace regarding the accident. You see, the accident was due to his negligence, as he was charged for a DUI. A year after the incident, he waited to hear from the court about his sentencing. The church prayed for our family, and his connection group also supported and prayed for him. He had a lot of support, and several people went to court with him. When his sentencing date came, the judge sentenced him to 12 years, serving seven in jail and five on probation.

I was devastated and not expecting that ruling.

Again, I believed in God to answer my prayers, and my prayer was that his sentence would be short. I felt like he had been through enough. Losing his daughter is something he will always live with. The same way God extends me grace every day, even when I feel undeserving, I wanted to impart the same grace in my son-in-love's life. While in court, my heart was heavy. It was like reliving the accident, the pain, and the memories all over again. Once my son-in-love was locked up, my daughter and her children moved into our two-bedroom apartment. We were empty nesters for quite some time, so we had embraced my daughter and grandchildren.

"God, help us all get through the challenges," I prayed.

Chapter Five

2014

With so many people in one small space, we needed to move from the apartment to a larger home. Interestingly, we had heard about a five-bedroom house for sale, so we went for it. Although the process took a minute to complete, we got the house and were in heaven with all the space we knew we needed.

Around the end of August 2014, my husband called me and said he was not feeling well. He did not go to work that day. I did not think much of it, so my daughter and I continued to attend our weekly line dancing class. We danced our hearts out. Over the weekend, I went to church, but John stayed home, yet I was not alarmed about him not coming because I figured he was still sick and needed time to recover.

On Monday, I went to work as usual, and while I was there, I called my husband to check on him. Sadly, he seemed to be getting worse. So, he made a doctor's appointment. The appointment was routine, just checking him out and eventually giving him pain medicine. However, when John arrived home, he started to feel weak and wanted to rest. He was in pain around his abdomen and lower back when he went to the bathroom. Although I had experienced kidney issues, I was not necessarily scared about his kidneys because my mind was not going there. I was more so thinking he had some sort of flu.

A few days later, we had plans to go out for our anniversary, to enjoy dinner and a movie, but John saw blood in his urine. Instead of our date, we went to urgent care, and they determined he had and urinary tract infection, letting him know that men rarely experience one, but they are possible.

During the next week, John did not have an appetite, and he started having a lot of pain in his lower back area again. We simply did not understand what was going on with his body. We contacted his primary doctor and told them he was getting worse. So, they prescribed more pain medicine. The pain medicine helped, but John became weak and lethargic and threw up his food. I called the doctor again, telling them about my husband's symptoms, so they had him come to the doctor's office. The primary doctor was not there, but the doctor we saw told John that he would schedule a CT scan, and off we went to the nearest Kaiser location.

A few days later, my husband's doctor told us to come in to discuss the test results; however, the doctors did not know what to make of what they saw on the scan. It looked like a mass in between his stomach and spine, and they wanted to do a biopsy because they thought it was cancer. Once his doctor received John's biopsy, they needed to send it to John Hopkins to run some tests, which meant waiting about five days before those results would come back. Hearing the word "cancer" was debilitating, but we wanted to know the root of his pain, and to wait five days was challenging, to say the least.

Each day, John became more uncomfortable. He could not sleep at night, and when he did fall asleep, he would wake up in excruciating pain.

On the way home from work one day, I decided to take John to the hospital because his pain was too much for him to handle. On my way to the hospital, I received a call from his doctor. The results came back. He did not have cancer. Praise God! The doctor at the hospital ran more tests and discovered salmonella poisoning. The CDC got involved, trying to find out how he got salmonella poisoning. They went to John's job to investigate, and we received calls from the health department about the investigation.

As days progressed, and after several tests run by my husband's vascular doctor, he informed us that John had an aortic aneurysm and needed surgery within the week. However, his doctor needed assistance with the surgery, and the other doctor was unavailable for a couple of days due to previously scheduled surgeries. As we waited, each day was a struggle because my husband was in so much pain.

The day before his surgery, the high-dosage pain medication he was given was not working. Therefore, John had a painful episode. He had climbed on the top of the hospital bed rail, acting erratically. His abdomen pain was so excruciating that it was causing him to check out mentally.

The next day, surgery was scheduled for 11:00 am. I stayed with John until he went to sleep, and I left around 2 am. I arrived back at the hotel to catch a few hours of sleep so I could be there for John before he went into surgery. When I woke up, I noticed I had two missed calls, one around 5:30 am and again at 6:00 am. The nurse left a message letting me know that John had another episode, so the doctor decided to do emergency surgery because they did not want the aneurysm to burst. If it were to burst, he would die.

I was devastated, so again, I called my pastor's wife in my time of need. She reassured me that everything would be alright and reminded me that I could not do anything but get some rest and wait for him until he got out of surgery. So, I did just that.

Hours later, praise the Lord, the surgery went well.

Going through that ordeal was frightening, as the unknown is always unpredictable. Thankfully, my church family prayed us through, and we did not pass out. Praise God!

After one month, John was discharged from the hospital. Because of the salmonella poisoning, he had to take antibiotics through iv therapy twice a day, every day, for 30 days. I had to be trained on how to handle his iv. I was still working, so I had to adjust my work schedule to take care of my husband, a duty I was proud to do.

Chapter Six

2016

Between my son-in-love's sentencing, the passing of my granddaughter, and my husband's surgery, I just wanted to fix things. I wanted everything and everyone to be okay. In thinking about life, I want to fix people and situations in general, not because I judge them but because I want to help. But I have learned that some things are not to be fixed, and if I can improve a situation, that does not mean I should. It does not mean I do not love them. Instead, I must give people to God, even those closest to me. On the flip side is the feeling of disappointment from not being able to help people.

Learning how to do it God's way made me feel like a punk yet Proverbs 25:2 reminds us that some things need to be concealed. God hides His wisdom so that we will seek Him. God knows how to handle all situations if you trust Him to fix them. Giving up that control is like giving up an addiction. It's about giving God the glory and not trying to fix something out of your control. God has opened my eyes to how much I was a fix-it girl. I believe God will give me things to help fix, such as people and situations, but a fruitful outcome will be with His leading, not mine. Learn to "Choose your battles." I am not to take on everything or everybody's issues and should not allow people to pressure me, either. I have learned to put it back in their court because I am not God. We are to cast our cares to Jesus. It is liberating to know that I do not have to fix everything, I must walk them through and understand that I cannot transform them on the inside. I cannot change their attitudes, nor can I heal them physically, emotionally, and spiritually; only God can. But I can be available to let Him use me. This requires me to put on God's full armor. Wearing spiritual armor means we know the truth, believe the truth, and speak the truth. If you are being attacked in health, finances, relationships, and self-esteem, know this is warfare. Are you putting on the full armor of God?

We are to proclaim the Gospel no matter how much resistance we face. We are not to waiver in our faith but to trust in God's promises no matter the storms that come our way. Our offense against the enemy is the Word of God, not our opinions or emotions. The many lessons learned about being Ms. Fix It have been challenging. You can come under so much pressure from people when you do not fix a situation for them. This proves to be difficult for others to process because some people perceive it as indifference. More importantly, it is not always about fixing someone, but leading them to Christ, showing them His ways in the Bible. Providing answers and comfort and listening are a part of being a believer, but when it becomes consuming or shouldering burdens, you must change. Something is wrong if you want it for them more than they want it for themselves. During this time, I was going into depression because I could not fix my issues or others.

"Is God not answering me?" I wondered, feeling heavy about life and loaded with doubt. "Do I matter? What is my purpose?" I often questioned.

In those moments of doubt, I knew I needed to pray. So, I would recite Isaiah 55:8-9 (NASB):

"For My thoughts are not your thoughts, Nor are your ways My ways," declares the Lord. "For as the heavens

are higher than the earth, So are My ways higher than your ways And My thoughts than your thoughts."

The year 2016 proved to be a year of lessons. I remember a day in which my feelings were hurt. I could not fix a situation I had messed up. I was going through what felt like every emotion. As I sat with my feelings, I realized I do not like to be wrong or mess up. My pride had been crushed. I needed to humble myself. I need to do so when I am right and wrong. I had been raked over the coals by my family because I messed up. But I had to face that I messed up and ask for forgiveness. Proverbs 29:23 reminds us that pride ends in humiliation while humility brings honor, and Proverbs 16:18 reminds us that pride goes before destruction and haughtiness before the fall.

I knew God was bringing balance to my life. He made me empathetic to help others. He was fine-tuning me through lessons of not needing to be accepted by others or needing to fit in. He molded me to stand out. My convictions are strong, and my integrity kicks in to make sound decisions. I am not better than anyone. I desire to do what pleases the Lord. I needed to learn how to relax on this journey with Christ.

Nothing moves faster or changes because I think it should. Life shifts because God is in control. The Lord has helped me not fix things through retaliation and isolation. I have learned not to let people keep me bound because they are bound. The best way to be released from manipulation is to pray for them. Suffering does not feel good, but it is good for you.

Chapter Seven

June 2016

Today, I got something accomplished. I was learning to follow the Holy Spirit, which is a life journey. Believers do not receive the Holy Spirit in one setting; He teaches ongoingly. For that, I am thankful. Moving with God will lead you to accomplish so much more in life. Your purpose becomes clear and fulfilling. It takes you out of yourself and your comfort zone.

Today, I was scrolling through my phone and saw several friends' numbers from high school. In the past, we would reconnect and disconnect. With one particular number, I called my old friend and left a message. To my surprise, she called back in about 15 minutes. I knew God had led me to call her. She shared about her mom not feeling well and that her family members were not supporting each other. I felt her pain. I encouraged her to forgive and continue to do what she could for her mom.

That same day, I talked to another young lady. While at work, I happened to see her, and I heard the Lord say to buy her lunch. Although we did not work together, we worked at the same company, so it was wonderful to cross paths. That day, I had asked her what she was eating for lunch.

"Nothing," she said graciously.

"But I'm supposed to buy you lunch," I said. "The Lord told me so," I smiled.

Her face lit up, so I went to get her lunch.

I was asking God to use me every day to make a difference (M.A.D.) in others' lives. That day, I had learned to get my self-worth from God, not people, including not seeking accolades and praise. Still, I realized I wanted more, and that was peace and satisfaction, knowing that I was pleasing God and doing the right things for God, such as following the Holy Spirit and His voice. He is the standard I live by, not my own or others.

When you get to this place of peace and understanding, you must continue to step out and take the courage to obey God. Sometimes, it feels like you are the only one walking that path, no matter how many people you are around. Nonetheless, you still stand out in the crowd. Truth be told, I do not like standing out. I prefer to be behind the scenes. But I am feeling more that God wants to elevate me. I realized I must guard my heart, especially when I feel betrayed. I am asking God to help me do it His way. I want to be used by God. God is faithful to get us to where He wants us.

October 7, 2016

In my devotion, I was reading about being a warrior for God. The devotion was about Gideon. His family rejected him, and he did not see himself as a warrior but a failure. People rejected him. I related to Gideon. This lesson showed that God saw Gideon as a warrior and would lead the people to war and win (Judge 6).

While reading, the devotion mentioned how fear keeps you from moving forward because you will not fulfill what God has placed in your heart. So, I had thought, "What is keeping me from moving forward?" I heard the Lord say fear of lack. I had been struggling to trust God for our finances. I felt like we must've not been good enough, doing enough, or would not have enough. The Lord showed me my issue. The issue was not the money; it was my pride and independence from Him. He showed me I was prideful toward Him, not just people. Pride is what got Lucifer kicked out of Heaven. So, I started trying to justify my pride, and He showed me that I was trying to figure out life without Him. It would never be enough, no matter how much I made, because my dependence on God for everything was lacking. Only He can fill the voids.

As usual, He is always on time, especially as I faced a lesson-reaping challenge. I had sent a text to John to let him know that the car insurance would be canceled on October 9th due to a lack of payment. After I sent the text, I went back to re-read it. John texted back and said, "You sent this to ten other people."

"Oh, no!" I said aloud, yet quickly calming down because I realized those ten people were family.

"My bad. Disregard," I had texted them.

Within moments, I received three texts from people giving me money toward our bill, one of whom paid it off. What a beautifully gracious lesson I learned and that was to let pride go. Thank You, Lord.

Chapter Eight

February 2017

The Lord showed me that I was carrying an offense toward my children for deciding to leave the church we attend. I had always thought we were a H.O.T. family – honest, open, and transparent – yet their recent decision created a separation we had never faced as a family. The Lord showed me that I was looking at the situation from a leader's perspective and not a mother's perspective. He wanted me to be honest with myself that I was hurt when they moved on. It was tough letting go and trusting God's process, but we do not always know God's plans.

I read my devotion the next day, and Romans 12:15 popped up. I read about being happy with those who are happy and weep with those who weep. In my devotion, the writer shared how his daughter came home hurt that she did not make the color guard. When she got home, she went straight to her walk-in closet, sat down, and started crying. One by one, her family members sat with her in the closet and cried with her. They did not try to mask the pain, change the subject, or tell her to try another time. They let her grieve through her loss and disappointment.

One of the things the Lord showed me when we met with my family was that they needed to express how they felt. It looked like we were quick to defend other families and friends, and we realized we should have let our children vent. Now we understand why they thought we were taking the other side instead of theirs. Going through this helped me realize it's okay for people to express where they are, even to my discomfort. I do not have to fix it, and I do not have to change their minds about their feelings. God is the one that can change their hearts and minds.

On July 22, 2017, I was headed to a Prophetic Music conference in Tallahassee, Florida. On the road, about 30 minutes before arriving at our daughters-in-loves parents' home, I got a call from my sister, letting me know that our mother had passed. Although I knew she did not have long to live, I was not expecting that phone call. My mother was 83-year-old (lack of thriving), had no will to live and had no appetite. Her declining health was a wake-up call for my sibling. They did not want to be on drugs when my mother passed. God gave them grace and answered their prayers. They did not start off being my mother's caregiver, but they ended up taking care of Mom to the end. They now serve the Lord. My prayer for years has been for the Lord to let my mom see my sibling doing well before she left this Earth. He did that! Thank You, Lord. You have been so faithful to me.

During this conference, I was with my pastors, and they were having presbytery, giving the Word of the Lord to people. They gave me a word of encouragement and exhortation, and the following day after my mother passed, I received this word from God:

I am going to dig in your ear because sometimes people want to be "in the position," but sometimes, the position is of influence—the position is one of the right-hand person. You have been there to see what others have not experienced to maximize your experience as a servant, for God is preparing you for your next dimension in Him. So, do not reduce what He is doing in you to "just helping." (Who said you were just helping anyway?) That is development for where He is taking you because everybody on the team must be anointed, sure, confident, and walking in what God has said. Who placed limitations on you? Who told you that you could not be what they see in you? Deal with it and settle the score. You are not walking in your purpose because you have the wrong perception of yourself. Where did the inadequacy come from? Where did the insecurity come from? That season is over, and God is pulling the covers off of you. He will cause unrest in your life until you come into total alignment and agreement with what He has said. This is not the season to be in hiding. You will not hide behind your gifts and good service. What you are comfortable with, be all He has said because the blessing is in your total obedience. I am not impressed because you do half of what He said. Whatever you desire in your heart, do it well. This is a season of replacements where some folks in ministry have gotten comfortable. They have gotten familiar and do not see God like they used to. God is sending some replacements, and He is raising them up. You are one of those people. Be prepared to become proficient in your craft, so you step in where you need to be at a moment's notice. You've got the goods, so walk in it and deal with your insecurities. Deal with your perception of yourself. This is what God says about you and what He says is the truth.

Job Promotion

August 2017

In 1996, I started working at Georgia Tech in Directory Services. For 24 years, I answered calls from all over the world and transferred them to various areas. In 2017, I was offered an IT Support Professional I position, and I accepted the job. Two years later, in 2019, we experienced departmental changes, a reunification, which resulted in another promotion, now working as IT Support Professional II. There have been some changes along the way, and I did not realize the adjustments I would have to make once I accepted the promotion. As I was facing challenges at work, I had a conversation with the Lord. He prompted me to go online and look at my pay stub to see how much I was making. I realized I had received a raise. I was convicted to stop complaining. The Lord began to speak to me, telling me I was ungrateful because I had been complaining and wanting to quit. I strongly expressed my opinion in the meetings, letting management know we needed more support because we were often accused of not responding to customers or answering calls. I told my manager we would love some positive affirmations about what we were doing well. However, the Lord began to tell me that I do not need to speak up in the meetings like that anymore because I had made errors myself, and I need to listen and learn from my mistakes. I had to decide to change my attitude and how I was thinking and talking about my job. I've struggled with not being certified in the IT field. I had insecurities about my performance, but the Lord said to me, "But I opened the door for you. I gave you this job. Do you think I would put you in this position to fail?"

He was causing me to grow and not live in a place of fear and defeat, but a place of faith, teaching me not to give up in tough times. I needed to remember who gave me this job and work unto the Lord. That meant I must talk to God every day about my job, bringing Him every concern and every insecurity. I had decided no more complaining but to thank the Lord for the opportunity. God was changing me and how I saw myself working as an IT Support Professional II. He showed me my skills, abilities, and the favor over my life. He was making me a woman of great faith.

When everything looks like it is putting you down, God says differently. The love of our Father does not always feel good, but I was learning more about His love for me. It is not always about getting my way but what is best for my life.

Chapter Nine

January 2019

In January 2019, ten years after losing our house. My husband told me that we would move from the place we were renting to buying a new house in January, I heard the same, but we will be building our next house. In the meantime, John had been looking at this subdivision for about two years. In February 2019, we talked about moving before the lease was up. We let our daughter know we were moving, and she needed to find a place for her and her family to live. At that time, she and my son-in-love had to work through some things. We realized it was time for us to part ways, as we had lived together for five years.

My husband asked my son, John III, and Sequoya if we could move in with them. We wanted to save money to purchase a house. They said yes.

We went to look at houses in the same subdivision John was looking at, and we saw two properties, but they were sold. Then, we were told that they had one house that was not sold.

So, we wanted that one. Next, we connected to a realtor recommended by a friend.

When we called about the house, they told us that it was unavailable and there were no more lots available.

But God.

The agent helping us told John that the builder said when he removed the trailer off the land, we could purchase that property. We were in awe. The Lord reminded me that we would build our next house.

On June 26, 2019, we were told to turn in the paperwork within the next 14 days. We had a slight hold-up on locating some of the paperwork, but we found it. We were able to put money down to hold the property. We signed the contract and needed to have the earnest money for the house. We were contacted to come to the design center to pick out what we wanted in our new home. My, it was exciting.

As we got closer to close on the house, the process began to unfold unpleasantly. We received a call from a bill collector that we did not know existed. We addressed the debt, and it took our score up to what we needed. So, we were told that we would need to bring the closing costs, which were more than what they told us. We were devastated. The mortgage loaner officer working with us did not mention bringing a closing cost. He was going to pay it.

All that time, we were waiting and doing our part, but there was a chance we would not move into this house. We had to encourage each other and believe God to answer our prayers. The thoughts of retreating were overwhelming. We had become discouraged, contemplating just walking away from the deal. I had told John this was bigger than us, that God must do this. We continued to pay our bills and pay off debt.

The closing costs were more than we had, but the Lord told me to ask three people to help us. We were able to get it from one person and then a second person and we were the third person. We now had what we needed to give by November.

We decided to give an offering toward our financial needs. We needed a miracle that only God could provide. Shortly after that, John received a call from a coworker to look at some work for a potential client, someone that wanted their house painted. So, he provided a quote. Two days later, John got the job. John then contacted the guy he used to help him paint other big jobs. He told John he could do the job and asked how much he wanted for the down deposit. John told him $2,000.

He said, "I'm going to do better," and he gave him $3,000. We needed a certain amount, and God came through with miracle after a miracle.

After being in our new home for two months, my mom's house caught on fire. My youngest sister, her grandson, and youngest daughter were home at the time. That evening, her daughter got up because she smelled smoke. So, she woke her mom up, and they went downstairs in the basement, where the fire started in one of the bedrooms. My sister ran back upstairs to get her grandson and ran out of the house to call the fire department. Immediately after work, I went to their home to help move some things out and tried to figure out what they would do. They decided to live with John and me.

In May, after my sister, niece, and great-nephew moved in, we helped my niece get some things together in her life together, such as paying off debt, purchasing a car, and saving money for their new place. My niece had received some money to take care of personal things. About a week or two later, she was blessed with unexpected funds. She asked me to help her set goals, and she was able to do all the plans she wrote down on the board.

Weeks later, right before Father's Day, my niece was diagnosed which COVID-19. So, John and I had to isolate for 14 days. After finding out about my niece, I began to have a cough, but I thought it was just a cold, so I bought cough medicine and regularly took it. I went to work that Monday, but I felt lethargic. The next day, I felt the same way. I noticed I was getting hot and could not focus on my work. So, I decided to take off from work for a couple of days to get myself together. I noticed I was starting to experience severe symptoms. I was coughing more and started thinking I might have COVID-19, so I isolated myself from my husband. Shortly after that, my husband started coughing and was lethargic. At that point, we thought he might have it, too. Then, I lost my smell and my taste. By this time, it was the weekend of July 4th. I received a call from my daughter later that day. She wanted John and me to go to urgent care because I kept coughing continuously. Thank God my husband was strong enough to drive us.

When we arrived, the staff tested us for COVID. They also wanted to do an X-ray. It was a long wait, and it was freezing in that tent. I wanted to get home and rest. Come to find out, we were both positive. Also, when I was getting the X-ray, the doctor said they saw a slight bruise in my chest where I had been coughing. They gave me antibiotics to take for about two weeks to help clear up that area. So, I was relieved to know something was going on in my chest area due to the coughing from the virus. The cough was horrible, but my doctor said it was mucus or phlegm stuck in my throat. They recommended plenty of fluids. I did not have an appetite, but I knew I needed to eat to keep my strength. We took our vitamin C pills and zinc to build our immune system. We drank a lot of water, ate three meals each day, and rested. Over the weekend, I contacted my supervisor to let them know that I was out sick with COVID. The Lord blessed me to be paid while I was out sick.

Chapter Ten

June 2020

Years ago, as we casually dated, John had also dated someone else. When she found out that John and I were dating, we exchanged intense fellowship. She mentioned that she was pregnant with John's baby, and I told her I was pregnant with John's baby as well. When she told me she was pregnant, I thought she was lying. Fast forward, his son and sibling came to visit our home, and from a distance, I noticed his head looked like my son's head. I continued to walk toward the table, and as I looked down, I saw his foot which looked just like his dad's. At that moment, I knew he was John's son, but the tension between John and his son's family had not been addressed.

Ten years later, John attended a men's retreat, which gave him a spiritual awakening about a son that he denied for ten years. The Lord spoke to him, and his relationship with his son began to build. They visited one another and talked to each other often. Although they both knew John was the father, they wanted confirmation. So, in 2020, the Lord spoke to John on September 26th, encouraging him to text his son and share with him how he wanted to deal with the past so they could move forward. John decided to take a DNA test that day and coordinate a time to meet with his son. In October 2020, his son received the results and emailed them to John. Probability of paternity: 99.999%. In my heart, I always knew. Now, we are on this unique journey to further know John's son.

Chapter Eleven

A Different Perception on How You View life

Looking back at my life, I identify with being picked on by the enemy at an early age. I have dealt with not being enough. I have learned to stop comparing myself to others and to accept that God did not make me like someone else. Now, I find joy in serving the One who has loved me all my life, even in my mother's womb.

I had to choose to change my perception. Life can make you or break you. Many times, I wanted to give up, but I decided to press through and not pass out, though the different things I faced tried to define me and how I saw God, myself, and others. As long as I am alive, there will be challenges, victories, and disappointments. We must decide to keep our eyes on the One who died for us, who loves us more than anyone, and that is God, my Lord and Savior.

Let us press through our day-to-day life issues. We can do all thing through Christ who strengthens us. Change your perception and see yourself as a winner, no matter what comes your way. How you perceive the things you go through with people you are connected to will determine your destiny. Change your attitude! You are a conqueror. Believe in the Word of God. God said we can move mountains with faith the size of a mustard seed.

So, what mountain is standing in your way?

What do you need to do to change your perception?

What must you do to *Push Through?* Decide, *and Don't Pass Out*!

Keep the following Scriptures in your mind and on your heart so that you can change your perception and push through:

"A fool is in love with his own opinion, but wisdom means being teachable."

(Proverb 12:15 TPT)

"Keep your thoughts continually fixed on all that is authentic and real, honorable and admirable, beautiful and respectful, pure and holy, merciful and kind. And fasten your thoughts on every glorious word of God, praising him always."

(Philippians 4:8 TPT)

"Yes, feast on all the treasures of the heavenly realm and fill your thoughts with heavenly realities, and not with the distractions of the natural realm."

(Colossians 3:2 TPT)

"My fellow believers, when it seems as though you are facing nothing but difficulties, see it as an invaluable opportunity to experience the greatest joy you can! For you know that when your faith is tested it stirs up in you the power of endurance."

(James 1:2-3 TPT)

About The Author

Jacqueline Y. Howard has been happily married to Elder John Howard for 38 years. They have six children and 19 grandchildren. She is an IT Support Professional at Georgia Tech where she has worked for the past 26 years and gained a wealth of experience in supervision, conflict management, and project implementation. Howard is a motivational speaker, mentor, life skills coach, and interpersonal relationship builder, and certified life coach. Jackie is very active in the Metro City Church of Atlanta, Georgia. Currently, she serves as a leader on her pastor's team and teaches discipleship classes. She is also a leader on the prayer network and the women's network online as well as leads a small group of women for the purpose of discipleship and evangelism. Jackie takes great pride in problem-solving to make a positive, productive contribution to the families and residents in the Metro Atlanta area

Push Through and Don't Pass Out!

Let's Stay Connected!

 howardjackie12@gmail.com

Jacqueline Y. Howard

Push Through and Don't Pass Out!

Made in the USA
Columbia, SC
04 March 2025

54667584R00043